the acorn book
of *contemporary* haiku

edited by Lucien Stryk
and Kevin Bailey

acorn book company

This edition published in the UK by
acorn book company
PO Box 191
Tadworth
Surrey KT20 5YQ

e-mail:sales@acornbook.co.uk

www.acornbook.co.uk

ISBN-0-9534205-2-3

British Library Cataloguing in Publication Data.

A catalogue record for this book is available from the British Library.

First Published 2000

Cover Design by Chris Mulhern
Typesetting and layout by David Bird
Produced by Chris Mulhern and Pamela Russo
Printed and bound in Great Britain by
Biddles Ltd, Guildford and King's Lynn

for
Lawrence, Emily, Robert, and Hannah

Acknowledgements

The editors and publishers gratefully acknowledge permission to reprint poems in this anthology from the following:

Richard Bonfield: *Swan for all Seasons,* Coypu Publications (1997).

Alan Brownjohn: *In the Cruel Arcade,* Sinclair-Stevenson (1994).

David Cobb: *A Leap in the Light* (1991)
  and *Mounting Shadows* (1992), Equinox.

Andrè Duhaime: *Orange Peels* (translated by Dorothy Howard),
  Editions Asticou (1987).

James Kirkup: *Blue Bamboo,* Utsusemi, *Formulas for Chaos,* Hub Editions.

Roger McGough: *The Spotted Unicorn,* Viking/Penguin (1998).

Chris Mulhern: *Cloud Blunt Moon,* Iron Press (1994)
  and *Water,* acorn book company (1998).

Peter Redgrove: *My Father's Trapdoors,* Cape (1994).

Vincent Tripi: *White,* Swamp Press (1993).

Vasile Spinei: *The Monk's Smile,* Editura Leda (1996).

Ikuyo Yoshimura: *At the Riverside,* Ko-no-Kai (1990).

And special thanks to the Contributors to *HQ Poetry Magazine,*
  Issues 1 - 24, 1990-2000.

Lucien Stryk is one of the USA's most respected poets. He has translated numerous works from the Japanese, including the poems of Basho (*On Love and Barley: Haiku of Basho*, Penguin Classics). He has previously edited *The Penguin Book of Zen Poetry* and is the professor of poetry at the University of Illinois.

Kevin Bailey is a poet and the founder and editor of *HQ Poetry Magazine*, the UKs first international poetry magazine to incorporate 'mainstream' and haiku poetry on equal terms. His poetry is widely published and translated into several languages.

Contents

Foreword

Every once in a while I remember strolling through Hagi-no-Tena, a garden in Sone, near Osaka, dedicated to the spirit of the great four of haiku, Basho (1644-1694), Buson (1715-1783, Issa (1763-1832), and Shiki (1867-1902).

On that lovely autumn afternoon, over-whelmed by clumps of chrysanthemums, bronze, white, purple, gold, ringed by bird-flutes in the pines, I tried to imagine how the great ones might have chatted on the nature of their art, and their differing approaches to it.

I wondered then, how listening in from so far in the past, they might have responded to modern writers of haiku. I feel they would have found it enriching to open up *the acorn book of contemporary haiku*, and browse through, page by page, country by country, stirred by exciting images.

I feel most of these poets might have been nurtured in the art by the great four, and other gifted voices from the Seventeenth Century to the present day. Surely, they heard Issa cautioning,

> *Never forget;*
> *we walk on hell,*
> *gazing at flowers.*

or, shared his grief, as he wrote of his dead wife and children,

> *Outliving*
> *them all, all -*
> *how cold.*

then, doubled in laughter at his,

> *I'm leaving -*
> *now you can make love,*
> *my flies.*

And, they must have learned the art of compression from Masahide,

> *Barn's burnt down -*
> *now*
> *I can see the moon.*

and understand why the word now is given a line of its own - for yes, haiku needs rhythms as subtle as the best of any poetry.

Perhaps the thought that Basho, haiku's most perfect artist, became a zen monk, established early in haiku's development, a strong link with that discipline. Zenshi Ichimi (Poetry and Zen are one), becomes a natural truth to a poet seeking the haiku ideal.

The writers in this anthology, whether consciously or not, live within this vision of that ideal - to integrate life with the art. Thanks to the sensitive awareness of what true haiku is, my co-editor, Kevin Bailey, has let into these pages, poems as outstanding as these;

freezing winter night
trees everywhere blossom
with stars

Kevin Christianson

Brooms
sweeping the sky -
the pines of Baguio

Frederico C. Peralta

LUCIEN STRYK
London, March 2000

Introduction

1. 'In a way all my work is founded on Japanese art...'
                                                     Vincent van Gogh

In the winter of 1885, Vincent van Gogh, in despair at his self-presumed failure to find an artistic style that would faithfully realise his vision of the world, took a poor room above a colour shop in the Rue des Images, an ordinary street in the commercial district of Antwerp. Undernourished and badly dressed, he naturally gravitated to the anonymity of the docks, where streetwalkers and cheap eating houses provided him with the little food, and human contact, that he wanted or could afford. He was facing a personal and artistic crisis that seemed unresolvable, when, by chance, he found on the way back to his lodgings, an unremarkable little shop that sold the most unusual prints - and at a price that even a starving artist could afford.

Made by Japanese artists following the styles of Harunobu, Horishige and Hokusai, these beautifully coloured wood-block prints had become so commonplace in Japan that they were used to wrap around their porcelain exports and had for decades been arriving in the major European ports, including Antwerp (with its long history of trading with Japan and the East), and sold as a by-product in the lesser art shops of London and Paris. The early Impressionist painters in France were the first to draw inspiration from these 'primitive' artworks. Whistler and Manet became imitators, and most of the artists that now figure at the dawn of Modernism enthusiastically took ideas from these Japanese prints and added them piecemeal to their art.

Isolated in his artistic Dutch backwater, Vincent bought print after print, and pinned them up all over the walls of his little room. From this time, up to his death five years later, these prints travelled with him, and were tacked up in every room he inhabited. What is so significant is that Vincent seems to have absorbed the essence of Japanese art in its entirety. The boldness of colour, the clarity of shape, clear lines and the cropping of scenes, and the dramatic use of unusual perspectives and lines of view. One only has to compare the vivid blue and green 'Irises' screen panel painted by Ogata Korin (which Vincent probably never saw) to his own flower paintings, especially the sunflowers, to realise how completely Van Gogh is a part of this Japanese tradition.

Vincent's forceful promotion to his contemporaries, of this

Japanese art of everyday reality and sensual vitality, percolated through the Western art world of the early Twentieth century. He became, posthumously, the first true 'Modern'.

2. *In the Eye's Jewel*

The chain-reaction of artistic influence and development is so often a result of chance personal meetings, associations and seemingly trivial twists of fate. This is well proved when we consider the weave of events that happened over a particular thirty year period.

In 1883, the questionable professional opinion of Dr. Gachet probably contributed to the death of his friend Manet (and later Vincent, in 1890). Consequently, in 1885 Manet's bereaved mistress and model, (and inheritrix of his collection of Japonaiserie), Mery Laurent, became the lover of the poet Mallarmé, whose Tuesday evening artistic gatherings (known as the *mardis*) held in his Rue de Rome apartment in Paris, drew in Verlaine, Debussey, Claudel, Gide, Valèry, and around them in lesser circles of association, Pissarro, Cezanne, Gachet and Theo van Gogh.

Mallarmé's relationship with Laurent resulted in a creative shift from 'transcendental' to 'human' Symbolism where, as he says, he wishes to recreate for the reader of his poems 'visual impressions and radiant feelings combined'; *The kindling of the ever inward fire / The only fundamental is renewed / in the eye's jewel full of truth or laughter...*

Mallarmé lectured at Paris, Bruges, Oxford and Cambridge, spreading the new philosophy of 'Modern' art, with its emphasis on the visual or written image containing its own resonant *symbolic* meaning. The co-mingling of Impressionism and Symbolism had an appropriately diverse progeny.

In 1907, nine years after Mallarmé's death, T.E.Hulme returned home to London from a continental study-trip, full of Mallarmé, Verlaine, and the 'Symbolist revolution'. He had experienced and absorbed at first hand a major phase in the development of the Modernist movement in the arts, and the evolution of Impressionism into Expressionism. In March 1909, after befriending F.S.Flint ('a man who knew more of contemporary French poetry than anyone in London'), they started an unnamed society which met for the first time at the Eiffel Tower restaurant in Soho. They discussed how the old poetry could be replaced 'by *vers libre*, by the Japanese tanka and haikai...' Flint says; 'We were very much influenced by Modern French Symbolist poetry'.

In April 1909, the young Ezra Pound attended his first Eiffel Tower meeting. Already exchanging ideas by way of a regular correspondence with William Carlos Williams, the eventual influence of Pound upon the poetry of the Twentieth century, for good or ill, is well known and does not require re-telling here.

In the spring of 1912, Roger Fry held a major Post-Impressionist exhibition in London; there were twenty-one Van Gogh's shown. That same year, in Cologne, one hundred and eight Van Gogh's were exhibited. Vincent's paintings and ideas had entered the general artistic consciousness, and by November 1912, the Imagist manifesto had been formulated by Pound and published in the March 1913 edition of *Poetry*. Imagism in Britain and America flowered briefly, and faded. Eliot and Williams grew on and away from Pound's initial influence - but in both of them the art of Post-Impressionism, Symbolism, and Imagism remained to regenerate, hybridized. For many years Hulme's work survived only as an appendix to Pound's selected poems.

3. The Traveller Returns

William Carlos Williams' *The Red Wheel Barrow* is slightly more than a haiku and less than a tanka. This poem was first published in 1923. Almost forty years later, in 1962, Williams published *Pictures from Brueghel*; a collection of poems so full of haikuesque units, it would be tempting to conjecture that in the year before his death he had returned to the very origins of his poetry.

It was a forty years in which styles of socio-political realism and rhetoric dominated, with rare 'Romantic' exceptions, the 'Classical' poetic mainstream. Ironically, during the same forty years in Japan, the Modernist movement, encouraged by Nishiwaki Junzaburo, set out to obscure the traditional Japanese poetic forms by embracing Symbolism, Dadaism, and all the other permutations of '-isms' coming from the West; thus closing a circle of cultural reactions that had begun decades before, with those discarded woodcut prints, flooding into Western ports. This, I realise, is a simplistic progression of ideas, but in Tabibito Kaerazu's *No Traveller Returns*, published in 1947, we have the unwitting essence of the new international spirit of haiku. Its one hundred and sixty-eight sections include a mix of informal haiku, tanka, and longer poems, all infused with images as clear as a Hokasai print and a spirit of Zen:

Above a grain field
where desolation grows,
a pitiable crucified man
wearing a straw hat from
Van Gogh's self portrait,
and a blue shirt,
this suspended Ecce Homo -
the colour of life's twilight
pierces him...
Here, a man
is attempting to say
something.

In 1951, Cid Corman founded the magazine *Origin*, re-seeding American poetry with the ideas of Pound and Williams, and encouraging a fresh appreciation of Imagism and Japanese forms of poetry. Slowly, through the gravitation of British and American poet-academics to Japan in the 1950's and 60's, there opened up a means of transmission by which a new wave of Japanese cultural influence (as significant as that effecting the visual arts of a century before) was able to break into late Twentieth century poetics.

By the the late 1960's, poets with their minds open to the inspiration and experimentation of international poetic trends, and able to draw from that confusion of influences, ideas relevant to their own poetry, quickly became aware that the clarity offered by the poetry of Williams, Nishiwaki, and Takehashi, suggested the way towards a new mode of poetic expression. Poets such as James Kirkup, Adrian Henri, George Seferis, and Alexis Lykiard explored the use of haiku in its pure form and included them in collections of their work. Poetry magazines and societies devoted to haiku were established in America and Japan during the late 1960's; notably *Modern Haiku* and Atsuo Nakagawa's *Poetry Nippon*. Lucien Stryk's classic *Penguin Book of Zen Poetry* was published in 1973, and under this slow heat of influence haiku magazines and societies began to proliferate around the world.

4. *A Strange and Happy Meeting*

There will always be the haiku purists. The haiku is a traditional poetic form native to Japan, and there it should, and will, be preserved. But when haiku and other Japanese verse forms have been mauled, digested, and regurgitated by their own poets, and cast out of polite and innocent national isolation to be preyed upon by Imagism, Symbolism, Minimalism, and a hundred and one other cultural influences, the beast we are left with has had to adapt to survive. It is notable that many non-Japanese haiku magazines try to protect the haiku like some endangered animal, by giving it only a little literary space in which to roam free of the predatory attentions of mainstream poetry. This is done quite appropriately in its native land, fused as it is with Zen philosophy and culture, but it is an insult to the nature of literary evolution not to allow the form to mutate and hybridize within whatever cultural habitat it has become established.

The validity of this argument is evident when we look at the poetry collected together in this book. If we read the haiku of Spinei, Krasinsky, or Ionel, we see the clear influence of Eastern Orthodox iconography; the Hellenic poets such as Seferis, Lykiard and Goumas cannot avoid some infusion of the Classical into their work; the American and Canadian poets such as Tripi, Rutter, Swede and Jorgensen easily adopt the ironic (and often 'homespun') tone, typical of so much 'New World' literature. Peralta, Forbes, and Prime represent, geographically, places scattered down the Western Pacific rim from Japan - a direct sphere of influence where there is a growing exchange of cultural ideas forming a Pacific 'identity', loyal to the more traditional form of haiku. Western European poets seem to be trying to effect a fusion of their own Symbolist and Imagist traditions, derived from Mallarmé, Rilke, and Hulme, with the idea of haiku. At worst this results in a colonisation of the form, but at its best, as exemplified by the work of Ricard, Russo, or Guiddicci, there is a unique cultural blending, creating a Post-Symbolist clarity of vision and ideas. The British, rather unexpectedly, form the most radical and least cohesive group, pirating haiku in many enriching ways. Bonfield, in his haikuesque poems, mixes the *Chansons bas* of Mallarmé with the haiku of Basho; McCall gets a Johnsonian humour into his Haiku Dictionary; Caley creates an inner sculpture; Cobb, and many of the other British poets included, express social anger and personal passion forthrightly enough to lift from them Alvarez's curse of 'gentility'. And at the most extreme edge of haiku literature, a popular poet such as Roger McGough can present his readership with a comic pastiche of classical haiku, confident that they will get the joke (demonstrating that an awareness, if not an understanding of haiku, has penetrated mainstream Western literary culture), and

Henry, with *Nuns in Milan Cathedral*, creates a poem describing the genius loci - a real and spiritual evocation of place; the poem defining a spontaneous creative response to insightful personal experience: a quality of Zen.

As the brightly coloured wood-prints of Japan fired the creative imagination of Vincent van Gogh and his contemporaries, and helped to launch the Twentieth century's great visual arts adventure (now so obviously spent), so contemporary haiku, in their diversity, have an equal potential to inspire and revolutionise the development of Twenty-first Century poetry. This book represents one small act in the genesis of that revolution.

5. *The New Gallery*

We are in the dark. An old film projector clatters. The screen before us flickers with black and white images: the bleak, lifeless panorama of the Somme with its mud-caked corpses; bulldozers driving a tumbling anarchy of bodies into the burial pits at Auschwitz; the sky over Nagasaki brightening; a naked little girl running down a road in Vietnam with a pall of blackness behind her. This is reality. This is horror. And how do the visual arts of this *fin de siècle* respond? With segmented animal corpses suspended in formaldehyde, soiled unmade beds, the pastiche of Keaton (or is it *Bunuel?*), and gigantic steel statues bearing down from public places with their dominating Stalinesque charm. What a hopeless and inadequate response to nearly a century of ugliness and brutality: how sad - how empty of the human spirit. Those few minutes of film say so much more. Surely it is time for the Arts to say; 'Look! We have come through...'

The poems in this book are a celebration of life, love, and beauty. They have a right to oust a vapid, despairing art. You have in your hands a twenty-first century art gallery. Do not just *read* the poems in this book, but *look* at each one of them as you would a painting or sculpture displayed in a bright spacious gallery. Let your mind stand before the poem and study it. Get the image and the idea of the poem working simultaneously in your mind. Realise it. See the word-picture in your mind's eye and absorb the emotions, light or dark, into your soul. And then, to quote Lucien Stryk, you may experience in these poems the qualities of the Zen aesthetic; 'simplicity, naturalness, directness, profundity... each poem with its dominant mood [of]: sabi (isolation), wabi (poverty), aware (impermanence) or yugen (mystery).' Walk slowly through the pages of this book. Take it all in. These poems represent the world as it really is. They can involve us all.

'All humanity, all nature simplified... This description does not tell you anything - but when one sees this picture, when one looks at it for a long time, one gets the feeling of being present at a rebirth, total but benevolent, of all the things one should have believed in, should have wished for - a strange and happy meeting of very distant antiquities and crude modernity.'

Vincent van Gogh, Auvers, June 1890.

KEVIN BAILEY
Bath & Swindon, March 2000

References and suggested reading.

SWEETMAN, David, *The Love of Many Things: A Life of Vincent Van Gogh,* Hodder and Stoughton, 1990.
BOSLEY, Keith, (Trans.), *Mallarmé - The Poems,* Penguin, 1977.
JONES, Peter, (Ed.), Imagist Poetry, Penguin, 1972.
TOMLINSON, Charles, (Ed.), *William Carlos Williams - Selected Poems,* Penguin, 1976.
HIRATA, Hosea, *The Poetry and Poetics of Nishiwaki Junzaburo,* Princeton University Press, 1993.
STRYK, Lucien, and IKEMOTO, Takahashi, (Ed. & Trans.), *The Penguin Book of Zen Poetry,* Penguin, 1977.

The Poems

High in the mountain
'Climb up here' calls
The bush warbler

Atsuo NAKAGAWA Nagoya, Japan

you suckle the baby;
pairs of swallows
hold back the wind

from the cemetary
the grinding
of an electric saw

tracks in the snow
I call them labyrinth
my father - trenches

the odd tapping
of heels... behind me
the blind woman

under the bush of lilac
the beggar counts
his coins

on my father's forehead
the flickering light
of the icon lamp

the hat thrust on
the handle of the pitchfork
covers the moon

in the corpse's
half-closed eyes
the flame of a candle

raindrops
coursing
on mother's wrinkles

one word
but so many varieties
of rain

faintest pink
blossom pales
into fog

solitary weekend
the cherry tree blown
frantically

David FINLAY London

Ephemeral Juxtaposition

This blue door
Has been waiting all winter
For the daffodils in the blue vase.

Rock Pool

All day
The man rests inside her

like a rock pool
Left by passing waves.

Perfunctory

If that was a kiss,
        So is dew
Melting on a lonely man.

Poppies

On the fields of the Somme
Perennially bleeding
A red mist hovers.

Between two showers
the blue summer sky is drenched
with a nameless scent

The grand piano
darkens the whole room. Only
its wide grin is bright.

At Olympia,
the cock's archaic cry
in the rising sun

A distant window
flashes its secret message
in the setting sun

Bluebottle flying
round the kitchen - the droning
chant of temple monks

Little stone *jizo* -
carried in my pocket, where
my hand can stroke you

What ghost is dancing
beyond the weeping willow?
- A quiet fountain

To build a new bridge
they cut down the apple tree -
how the torrent roars!

White ones and pink ones -
the chestnut trees in bloom -
O, Champs Elysees

Whale Haiku

The whale skeleton:
I kneel to pray in it, as
in a cathedral

Sunlight through pines
the dog's collar
jingling

Autumn twilight
more starlings scared up
with every step

David ELLIOTT Factoryville, Pennsylvania

In the soft sunlight
my shadow pulling me
to a shady place.

Under Orion
a shortcut through the old graveyard
savouring the frost.

Another robin in my mousetrap:
few of us fail to give
humanity a bad name.

late summer breeze -
leaves of my book turning
before they are read

the rising moon
full on my nape
the breath of a moth

arms round a fuchsia
he stands at the greenhouse door
sniffing for frost

homecoming:
a two-day growth of beard
bristles her nipple...

children asleep
after bedtime stories
sticky fingermarks

first day at school -
wind with the garden swing
all to itself

cracked sandals
in the porch since summer
filling with snow

the mist is rising
even
under the lowered
coffin

sometimes just one hair
fallen in a vacant room
will not be picked up

David COBB Shalford, Essex

Puddles -
seeing clouds drifting
below one's feet.

B. H. WELLS Southsea, Hampshire

the little girl's bubble gum
   explodes -
      summer moon

in the general direction
of the nuclear power plant
sunset

between the legs
of a mint-striped deckchair
blue water

after the goodbye kiss
the sweetness
of a russet apple

alone again,
the ginger cat
curls on the sundial

cleaning the bedroom -
the warmth of her shirt
left in the sun

my hand curves
    to fit your breast -
the windowsill, snow-laden

golden sun
still in the waving wheat
at twilight

Michael Dylan WELCH San Francisco

The old barn
  looks more like a tree
    each year.

The moon has risen again.
  Amazing, isn't it,
    how it never falls?

Wind down the chimney
))))))) all night long
pale plumes of wood smoke

First the aroma
as vacuum tubes heat
and then the music

Alec KOWALCZYK Albany, New York

Musica

The hand asks the heart
will friend or foetus phone first.
I hear a heartbeat.

The guitar is red.
We think around each other.
We hear rain coming.

The music enters,
weaves about my bones in tears.
I can hear me breathe.

You ask this tear its
meaning. How like nakedness
is my nakedness!

Fingers beat on wet
strings. There cries a single note.
I can hear silence.

Hill Track

Silence steals up like burned paper,
a black fleck rising
to the stillness of the elms.

Ahead the stony track narrows
and at the round brow
the sky backs off for miles.

Colin OLIVER Sudbury, Suffolk

stirring fieldmice
bending the ears of corn -
a wind from the south
          (after Tao Ch'ien)

unable to sleep -
the clank and rumble of trains
long into the night

argument over
         pushing past
the scent of her hair

abandoned -
the children's ride
plays out its tune

late afternoon sun
the shadow of the gravestone
slants towards my feet

Brian TASKER Frome, Somerset   39

hazy

summer's evening stillness
- looking back
the way we have come

in the powder blue sky
a faint sickle,
turning silver

snuggling against your back

in my hand
the plump, softness
of your breast

the crescent
and her shadow
complete

Chris MULHERN London

moonlight
a weight
on the old horse's back

seconds tick -
in the chapel of rest
a fall of petals

dew
on the scarecrow's face
dead white

snow falls -
mother's new grave
almost out of sight

under moonlight
the dead bird's eyes
are little lakes

flowers
to bring butterflies
to mother's grave

bitter cold
  the unfrozen center of the pond
    shudders

third hour of snowfall
the colour of silence
is white

sunrise
the fisherman's shadow stretches
across the river

the wind fiercest
in the maple that still
has its leaves

evening sunbeam too
lingers on the naked breasts
of the garden Venus

George SWEDE Toronto, Canada

Night Table

Here is part of you
While you sleep -

The small shine
Of silver earrings

Work Gloves

On the garden gate
Left here with me -
Shape of her hands

Baker

Kitchen spotless -
But flour
On her lips

They leave their fortune cookies
on the table
old nuns.

First warm day,
the deaf couple signing
with their gloves off

Outside the hospital
headlights of a locked car
growing dim

Stargazing
mouth after mouth
full of blackberries

Hazy moon:
a square of flattened grass
below the army blanket

Blind mother
nursing longer than usual
under the cherry blossoms

Alphabet soup:
tongue on the s
when my ex calls

The white kitten
playing & playing
with the faded cherry petal

City visit...
my mother taking confession
in her native tongue

Yard sale:
my next door neighbour pauses
by the nightie

Christmas balls
shimmering in the window of
the strip joint

Grandpa's telescope
late at night points
toward the nursing home

Vincent TRIPI San Francisco   45

I am old. And now
  face eternities of stars
    as a speck of dust.

Let me cherish still
  this fake-ivory Virgin
    warmed by my fingers.

Why long for a storm?
  This rose breathes its best self
    in a quiet air.

Your bright mind whirr's on.
  I am the worn patterned carpet
    to be cleaned of dust.

Still in my garden
  I bend to pluck a weed but
    see its smiling face.

Harold MORLAND St. Annes-on-Sea, Lancashire

In the garden of Salah
The silence is soothed
By the whispered lisp of leaves.

A new-born grasshopper -
on its antenna
tiny morning dew

A secret
kindles in my heart -
the red yew-berry

My old diary -
a bookworm devours
the passion it keeps

The youngest daughter
gone off to be married -
one last persimmon

A white heron
soars upward - each cloud
becomes a bird

Snake gourd
over the gateway
to a deserted shrine

Keiko KAKAMI Gifu, Japan

The Zen of Bowmanship

Get to know the breath
  as you'd test the bowstring first
    take yourself in hand.

Weigh your intention
  and if the aim falls too low
    wait till tomorrow.

To put you in heart
  fill the lungs to their deepest
    then make for the mark.

With forceful vigour
  you draw the bow back at last
    a godlike figure.

Breathing comes easy
  the strength flows trembling through you
    let the arrow fly.

It takes you with it
  breath and the will are one
    I is left behind.

translated from the German by Yann Lovelock

Ilse FISCHER-REITBÖCK Germany

threading our way
through a dappled forest -
birdsong; thin as lace

Fred SCHOFIELD Leeds

Night-Moves

To evade
the gamekeeper,
I wade
a little deeper.

Bewitched
whispers
of the flyfisher's
roll & switch.

Corona Borealis -
you might
say the night
was made of this.

A moorhen dives.
Ripples spread
To the ends of the earth

Aasha HANLEY Panaji, India

Two old pines
Lean against each other
Weighted down with snow.

Cloudless dawn;
Drone of a fisherman's boat
crossing the lake.

A day so still...
Reluctant to dip an oar
Into the water.

A seaplane landing -
the sound not reaching us yet;
faint light of dawn.

Fountain in the Mall;
Delighted, the old vagrant
dunks his head in.

Evening orange grove
The wedge of moon
caught in both your eyes

Mission chapel:
an offering of flowers
in a Coke can

Through the opera glasses,
a glimpse of tongue
delighting a nape

punters on the Isis:
condom foils
floating in their wake

Even in the napkin ring
around the checkered cloth
You see her waist, that dress

Christmas puppy
leaves toothmarks on your hip
like I do

Heidi TRILLING Menlo Park, California

Solstice evening -
washing dries in
sweet woodsmoke

Laughing at ourselves -
so stoned
on love and LSD

She says that she dreams
of another man, she says
nightmares are nothing

on the beach
old hippies
building sand castles

every day now
wisteria buds
a little fatter

hippie reunion -
the unfamiliar smell
of his deodorant

on the toilet
Stryk and Ikemoto's
Zen Poetry

tax forms complete -
her reluctance to affix
a *Love* stamp

Linda Jeannette WARD Coinjock, North Carolina

Birthday Gift

Today I give you
a blue wood egg-cup
for your yolk to run
its yellow down

From *A Year*

Winter

After a night of storms,
unbroken by the wind,
snowdrops.

Spring

The earth bears
everything,
even your sadness.

Summer

When the page was blank
no one thought, suddenly
a flower will appear.

Autumn

You hurry home
to match the landscape
to your box of colours.

David LINDLEY Long Ichington, Warwickshire

Love Play

Silence, and I watch
The soft cascade of her hair
Shimmer in the dark.

She is naked now
and the rose hue of her breasts
tints a gift of pearls.

Ingratitude

Thrown on nameless junk
In a forgotten attic,
A doll, doomed to stare.

seated at her old TV,
Great-grandmother chuckling
at the blank screen

seeking answers,
I keep getting none
from my answer machine

beside the Buddha
meditating on the shelf,
the cat, daydreaming

after that party
teeth marks - but whose? -
on my bottom

you and I silent,
between us on the sand
a shattered seashell

William WOODRUFF Pasadena, California

you will not turn to stone
carefully let me touch
your naked breast.

I hear the magpies
and you you have given me
this sense of longing.

what is in my heart?
you follow the line of trees,
on their bark an x.

look: chrysanthemums
the woman with the Greek name
smiles beyond my soul.

No Reply

I telephone home
Knowing you're not there, then wait
Imagining how

Long it would take you -
From garden, kitchen, bathroom -
To come to the 'phone

Longer, to allow
The thought of you at the door,
Fumbling for the key.

Tom VAUGHAN Kampala, Uganda

Secret Service

Internuncio
delivering messages
between silent lips

innocent sleeper
do you dream of paradise
when you shall wake?

the intelligence
of such beauty informing
that lust may be love

the uncertainty
of sure knowledge of who is
indefectible

I speak to the flowers.
They react, calmly,
beautifully. I speak
to you. You are away.

The poetry of deprivation,
the bare page
marking
your absence.

Michael KELLY Hull

too many vows broken -
between the rounds of spring rain
bullfrog

through stop signs
speeding the forest curves
to catch the moon

she calls
at the end of a working Sunday
to have me watch the snow

tilting into sleep
the music
from a distant fairground

fussing the foxglove,
a bee, working upwards, finds
the last flower too young

D. J. PEEL Birmingham

Birth -
lips parted
in surprise

A teaspoon
still rocking
on a white saucer

Childhood:
a ladybird crawling
in a closed jar

Last night's wet bus ride -
I would swear it was Turner
but she says Seurat

Aie! Home once again
Unyielding, the rusty lock
Then thirty-four stairs

Nothing to be said -
look at this flowering plant
and those soaring larks

George SHERIDAN Deia, Mallorca

open again
lips on a tea cup
blossom

Werner REICHHOLD Gualala, California

Changes

I sense a movement
At first only the leaves shake
Summer is leaving.

Cuckold

2-15 a.m.
Your footsteps in the street below.
I begin to practice the sound of sleep.

M. J. MALONE Boston, Lincolnshire

under my touch
    however gentle
        your nipples
bunch into fists

rear-view mirror -
    your eyes
        past me
looking for the fast lane

between the question
    and the reply -
sunlight on a few leaves moving

    one more day wasted -
the children's tin wheelbarrow
    brimming rainwater

Free of itself
the song
of the skylark.

Looking at
the wrinkles in my shaving mirror
I work up a lather

It's so cold
even the dahlias are shivering
in the breeze

Cy PATTERSON Consett, Co. Durham

Sky

A blue sky

flows on the sorrel -
she
a secret smile.

Carnival

I told the shop-owner:
give me a mask
since this one I have
does not please me.

translated from the Maltese by the author

on the washing line
her bra supports
the crescent moon

waiting...
her train
six butts late

on the iron fence
a single glove...
waves

forgotten gateway...
sycamore saplings
passing through

David WALKER Woolhope, Herefordshire

whisper of wind
  leaves brushing leaves
  as they fall

arm in arm
kicking through autumn leaves
my new friend and I

imprinted
in each new Aspen leaf
  the tree

first December snow
husband sweeps aside
the postman's footprints

Jean JORGENSEN Edmonton, Alberta

Hunter's moon
car in neutral
sneaking in

at dawn
the rocking chair still quivering -
the long night

she leaves the crowd
to watch
departing geese

Melissa SCANLON Broomall, Pennsylvania

In Monet's garden
the Japanese bridge bows low
to the floating lilies

Bathing in bubbles
my breasts turn into mountains
glistening with snow

Pam PENNY Caterham, Surrey

freezing winter night
trees everywhere blossom
with stars

Kevin CHRISTIANSON Cookville, Tennessee

miner's wife
first labor pain -
the pit siren

tree shadows
across the chess-board -
unfinished game

autumn burial -
the key at the door
so loud...

There is no argument
about the resurrection
of a snowdrop

After the sightless
blizzard
clear blue sky

Earth is a brief
shadow
on the face of the moon

Take a fistful
of sea,
it will make no difference

Robin IVY Cambridge

Casting Nets

A dripping sky came up with the nets
The fishermen were blue all over.

translated from the Turkish by Feyyaz Fergar

coming going
coming going
the sea ... the sea

full moon
death row inmate
hangs his shadow

sweat to sweat
sheet to sheet
eye to eye

hips swaying,
she leads him
to the sea ...

Sheldon YOUNG Montreal, Quebec

Nomad

Alone
on the beach -
each wave
a crowd
applauding
its own surge.

Winter Blues

I am
not sad -
my tears
are snowflakes
melting on a lash.

Shy

That silver birch
is conscious
of her curves.

She trembles -
autumn winds
will strip her bare.

the small gasp
in the throat of a lover.
No going back

Giles GOODLAND Oxford

Afterwards
searching together
for your stockings.

How ostentatious
those fingernails painted black
touching white orchids.

The Old Jewish Cemetery, Prague

A sea of gravestones.
Not waves but our hearts breaking
in this summer sun.

At dusk the whistle
of that lonely train disturbs
the quiet valley.

Robin BRUMBY Taunton, Somerset

Dusk
amber fog
of cigar smoke

Sickle moon
the colour of champagne
in a crystal glass

A lover's tiff -
what's left of it, apple peel
on side plates

Sweet peas endure among
tombstones - eyes of melted
lead in slumber

End of siesta -
rising, a scarecrow
in underwear

Francis ATTARD Marsa, Malta, GC

A lizard scrabbling
its feet, trying to run on
a marble gravestone.

The hour has not come
for high tide to wash away
a dead cat's maggots

Snake

Clinging together -
two little girls staring at
a snake in the grass

A Propos de Nice

1

After Matisse:
picnics beneath olive trees;
the Sunday light cuts shadows
like painted paper.

2

A mackerel sky
above fishing boats;
Dufy waves
feather the bay.

3

Nouveau riche
against the night
yellow lights
gleam on the bosom of the Corniche.

4

Beignets, Socca, Bagne Cauda:
tastes bright as bougainvillaea,
the night smell of datura.

for the River Mersey

today it is a yellow river
no moon
no drunk poets drowning.

for Elizabeth

morning:
your red nylon mac
blown like a poppy across Hardman St.

Hoyku

my spelling atrocious
my maths even worse
spend summer writing hoyku

Mike HOY Sheffield

tobacco smoke curls
upwards to the Expelair
like Salome's veils

lunchtime sandwiches
in the Recreation ground
starlings sound like phones

London haikuists
count syllables differently
to haikuists here

the blackbird as usual
when I was about to
buttonhole God

all night the trains
shunting into the station
WSW wind

in the taxidermist's window
like a crippled parasol
the old blue toucan

Seeking good news
I watch the lines on my palm
taking new turns

In the barber's yard
grass
gone to seed

Autumn sunset
- bailing colors
out of the boat

His burial day
- the gravedigger's hut
shrouded in mist

Matthew LOUVIERE New Orleans, Louisiana

dwarfed
by a Norfolk pine
the evening star

Patricia PRIME Te Atatu South, New Zealand

ancient headstones
the names and numbers
worn to mutters

a beetle
has the motel pool
all to itself

from 'Paris'

parkbench
lovers pantomime
the Kama Sutra

evening
a cat walks home
across apartment roofs

a short-legged mutt
trots by the Seine
carrying a rock

William HART Montrose, California

In the copse; no sound,
except the sniffing of the dog,
and the anger of fallen elms

Dried in the flames of
this amber season; the pale
face of chamomile.

My hair still falling:
by the way, a confusion
of drying grasses

On this old sick bed,
seeing you only in dreams,
I fall with the rain

lightning all last night -
perfect fish with open mouths
drift dead on the pond.

wasps cling to the pears
like sailors to the wreckage -
a cold Autumn wind.

touching her hand once -
the coolness of Greek temples,
a respite in shade.

The Jasmine

Whether dark
whether light
yet white
the jasmine.

from 'Haiku'

Thoughts
carrying her breasts
in the looking-glass.

Nude girl -
the seeding pomegranate
was crammed with stars.

This pillar has a hole,
it's a secret worth seeing
Persephone.

translated from the Greek by KB

George SEFERIS Athens, Greece

An Arrangement

You laugh at my flowers.
Do you not think the absurd
Has a certain charm?

Ronald TAMPLIN Ankara, Turkey

outside chapel
lovers sharing
the gift of tongues

a late daffodil
arrives in my back garden
puffing and blowing

sipping pale sherry
her words
colour his cheeks

fifth drink
ask me again
the meaning of life

in the silence
of the garden
breaking wind

birdsong
now fills the space
the party left

John ARNOLD Crowborough, Sussex

Be gentle with your guest,
flowering plum-tree:
this baby sparrow knows
no other home.

Full moon reflected
in a temple pool -
don't be jealous
water-lily.

Cherry blossom
on high branches -
the scent carries
for miles and miles.

Kevin DAVIES St.Albans, Hertfordshire

Voices of wild geese
so closely intermingled
as if wing to wing

Leaving the castle
one cherry blossom petal
still drifting on air

A beautiful girl -
fingering the brim of her
rice-planting sedge hat

*translated from the Japanese by James Kirkup and
Makoto Tamaki*

Seishi YAMAGUCHI Tokyo, Japan

this summer night -
she lets the firefly glow
through the cage of her fingers

Rather than follow
Basho's footsteps north, I rock
my baby to sleep.

May morning greenfly
in my pink lipstick, you chose
a beautiful death

Susan KERR London

behind the tractor
gulls like spoilt children
screech their hunger

a rare night of spring
I drop my pen and take up
love like a new task

against the cold,
we lie together - like spoons
old friends in old skin

Michael FACHERTY Kidmore End, Oxfordshire

Remembering last
summer's infidelity:
your tongue in my cheek.

Sheila GLEN BISHOP South Petherton, Somerset

Windmill
grows old
but not the wind

Setting sun
pulls its shadows
over the horizon

The evergreen tree
longs
to be naked.

A small jar
has bent
the goldfish

The bee kisses
the dying rose
goodbye

The sun is a beehive
rocked in the forest-bear's paws -
drunk, the final honeyed ray.

translated from the Russian by KB and the author

Arseny KONETSKY Moscow

In the plain vase
the forgotten sunflowers
turn to the light.

The high mountains.
Sometimes, the echoless
sound of a cow-bell...

Gazing at the moon
one realises that she
has come quite a way...

Under its weight of
years, a wall, crowned with ivy
slowly crumbles.

Daniel RICHARD Paris, France

Lantern on an old road.
It gathers around
so much night.

Nicolae IONEL Iasi, Romania

Here, not one plant,
not one animal -
        only stone and light.

Beside the fire,
silent vigil: a book
        and thoughts of you.

Cat in the dark:
two blazing eyes
        fixed on the moon.

translated from the Italian by James Kirkup

Three Full Moon Haiku

Low moon over sea.
Tall masts swing in the harbour
and play ball with it.

Moon so magnified,
coming from afar. What a
night for goalkeepers!

Blue sky. But the moon
all morning, like a dunce ghost,
outstays night's seance.

Dannie ABSE London

Paros Haiku

Bucket down a stone well -
      Hear the morning
            splinter into water!

mind your manners
little sparrows
I've just washed these quilts

strange
this house
not one nail mine

returning
along an unused path
wild strawberries

NIKA Calgary, Alberta

Sunburnt cheek
from watching the
geese go west.

the fox turns -
his eyes catch fire
in the dusk

moonlit breasts -
why does the pillow melt
under my hand?

Tessa ROSE Cambridge

As I swim
this water that drowns
has a fragrance

As fish gently pass
the full moon shivers back
into perfection

no wind today
on the fox's head
a blackbird in full song

An adder glides away -
the air is suddenly sweet
with violets

White birch tree
brushing another tint
on a spring cloud

I will take a nap
in this heavy shower of white
mountain cherry petals

Slowly I soak
my painful hands
in the hillside spring

Tadao OKAZAKI Fukushima, Japan

A hand from the water.
Circles out.

To find another stills
and clarifies the world.

*

Old vessel
of blue we hold to

to the end where all
we've emptied fills.

*

A moon to read by.
Gulls trail in

a line of broken shadows.
Every tide a text.

Brooms
sweeping the sky -
the pines of Baguio

Sunrise
temple flowers on wet grass
soot on mother's face

Christ's statue -
a bird perched on His head
pulling out thorns

Frederico C. PERALTA Quezon City, Philippines

generations buried -
from tombstone to tombstone
the dragonfly

a year older -
wild grasses where
the stream used to be

soaring eagles
    so many layers
        of sky

snowing again
    in this constantly turning
        paperweight

Phyllis WALSH Richland Center, Wisconsin

Child's Play

Peddlybikepeddlybike
Peddlybikepeddlybike
With the biggest, kindliest
Paternal
Smile on his face and
Laughter heating mine
Peddlybikepeddlybike

hand
on the hot lightbulb

and the shadow of the hand
filling this room

and the shadow of the hand
covering my face

and the eyes
that burn

Colin SAVAGE Sudbury, Suffolk

from *Lepidoptary - X-Ray Haiku*

everyone wears this
internal waistcoat, with chain
and ticking fob-watch

like some butterfly
in negative, wings parched-dry
with spar-white markings

Nabokov or E
-lizabeth Bishop's *Man-moth*
scorched to a pale fire

on a kimono.
Two geishas kiss a mirror
and are each other

into himself. Be
-hold, bleached Anorexia,
the Goddess of ribs

Matthew CALEY London

I look at my scar
remembering dark crimson
of autumn roses.

My blood is light,
the colour of cranberry juice,
a young woman says.

dining room table
a deserted cigarette
burns itself to death

this drizzle, these scores
of rivulets, sluicing down
city umbrellas

people on the bridge
behold their own reflection
rippling in the lake

Peter COWLAM Totnes, Devon

Trotting along,
side by side with the stray dog -
Wintry evening.

On an autumn morning
hairs, windows, grass -
all frost white.

My lonely cry
on the desolate shore...
Et tu, moon?

Growing old together;
asters and fresh maple leaves
in one vase.

Fractured on glass,
into my poor room
the smell of rain

End of October;
the Autumn horde gathers
on wet grass

translated from the Russian by KB

Michael KRASINSKY Moscow

first letter of the year
the stamp
an extinct bird

Summer vacation -
a single butterfly fluttering
in the piano lesson room

before the storm
all things living
in sudden silence

the first day of autumn
a single feather rolling
on the Tatami floor

junked car
side mirror reflecting
rainy sky

cultivator
along the highway, slow
as a pregnant woman

Ikuyo YOSHIMURA Gifu, Japan

Her speech is crystal -
A parade of little gems
Hide under her tongue

Rosemary ROWLEY Blackrock, Dublin

Selected from 'The Haiku Dictionary'

FOREMOST

by speed and cunning
to have outwitted millions
of our kindred sperms

JEALOUSY

guarding one's own love
as if it were something that
could be found again

LOVE

why the same word for
I love bananas as for
I love you or God?

NOSTALGIA

sunlight reflected
from the windows of a house
where we used to live

SPRING

    rooks lumber about
aerodynamically
unbalanced by love

THE UNIVERSE

    to understand it
hold a small bird on your hand
that is the centre

VINEGAR

    in glorious summer
the rancid sound of magpies
stealing my cherries

Philip McCALL Romsey, Hampshire

shifting winds
the gull
resumes its glide

mountain climbing
a solitary flower
pure white

jutting rock
the waterfall's two paths
to a quiet pool

Francine PORAD Mercer Island, Washington

still time
still light
one whisper for another

no one moves -
the winter evening
darkens the room

another room -
the song she sings
to herself

Success

i

I was invincibly attracted to her;
Only an abyss can exercise such fascination.

ii

I paused under a locust-tree, lighting a cigarette:
The water has our mark on it still.

iii

She told me at night, the time of living breath;
We took a shower in perfect darkness.

iv

Was that the distant roar of lions
Or the sound of the clouds travelling?

v

When a pregnant woman bows to an idol
The unborn child bows as she does, within the temple.

vi

So I went out and walked around the lake again
To listen to the sky; approaching thunder
Printed its paw-marks across the water.

Peter REDGROVE Falmouth, Cornwall

a slight drizzle -
the axe handle glistens
over split logs

fresh from the bath
she leans - two drops of water
catch the light

in nothing
but that blue silk dress
- dancing with others

see how the coastline
exactly fits the ocean
all the way along

under buddleia
tired of butterflies
a curled up cat

David STEELE Elmham, Norfolk

Like a neutral card from Smiths
Detail: Waterlilies (Monet)
I leave this poem
blank for your own message.

Andrew NIGHTINGALE Mullion, Cornwall

A Bundle of Letters

If the band should snap,
the room would fill with voices
flickering like birds.

Inheritance -
cigarette smoke still clings
to my father's books

A cracked soap
preserves the last
dirt from your hands

Nick PEARSON Bridgnorth, Shropshire

in the cinema
the worn-out secretaries
their lips like glow-worms

from 'Orange Peels'

she shakes the snow
from her unbuttoned coat
     a nipple

 red light
sloshing of the gasoline
     in the tank

    shivers
what's your nail writing
 on my sunburnt back

André DUHAIME Canada

Above the rooftops
Slate blue.
The night sky.

Sickle moon
Yes.
Sharp-edged.

Girl in an old pub photograph

Our eyes met
Across a crowded room
Across a hundred years.

Yes

In her Summer's dress

Yes.

James MORRIS Barnsley, Yorkshire

days without music
are like sons without mothers
or dried up oceans

there are as many Jews
hidden in the Spanish soul
as stars in a clear night

I know of a man who
slept with Garcia Lorca
and forgot all about poetry

Here, on the fourth floor,
The vending machine works
Harder than I do.

Vestibule Haiku

Ground.

Plug, in an orange
Socket, turns a tape. Girl clerks
Proffer pens and smiles.

Mezzanine.

Use-less hall space; glass
Restaurant doors, sheets over
The band's bright weapons.

First.

Still you can't see sky.
A person from Porlock: *Am
I disturbing you?*

Second.

With signs, a 'Plan of
Evacuation'. Useful!
Blue plug-socket here.

Third.

Miniature ferns
In a chipped bowl; one glass door,
Out of two, missing.

Fourth.

Green ashtray grained like
A breakwater. Carpets, clean.
Laurel in a pot.

Fifth.   Sky. A cloud looks through
            Lace drapes; lift-buttons bleached and
                Hollowed by fingers.

Sixth.   Two old men in hats,
            Awkward with a lift arrived
                Too soon. Carpets? Stained.

Seventh.   A wall clock wrenched out:
            A rose in a jar wilting
                Faster than its leaves.

Eighth.   The band-leader's room.
            I know, seeing him go there
                (All his summer life).

Ninth.   The last drone and gulp
            Of the slow lift. I tread on
                Carpets that fly.

Roof Terrace.   What you feel, here you
            Feel it: scared; free; bigger than
                Tree, cart, ball, church, plums.

Alan BROWNJOHN London   149

Tentatively, you
open the door. The room breathes
a sigh of relief.

serenity
three saffron monks
sipping green tea

as dusk falls
the sound of oars
rippling the river

dementia ward
conversation fading
to a line of dots...

first night of autumn
the moon and pumpkins
    face to face

 alone in the room
the blinkless eyes
    of the dolls

Lequita VANCE-WATKINS Carmel, California

January. Stoking the
dying embers. Her bike
clatters down the alley.

On the riverbank
after the flood subsides
sanitary towels.

The scent of old wine.
Fallen elderberries ferment
on the footpath.

Spectrum

VIOLET

valley where making
remains a realm of mystery
cutting off from time

INDIGO

into the brain itself
constants through scent
a necessary fiction

BLUE

bird butterfly and bee
each see the same colour
differently than we

GREEN

ground water beneath
anticipation and recall
fast young horses

YELLOW

years later small
glimpses of horizon lines
through apple branches

ORANGE

oppressive summer
so stripped of nuance
shielded from easy sound

RED

reading in too much light
close-ups of the surface
glow of a full moon

Nightwater passes under the mill -
the land follows more slowly.
Upstream and still, a liquid star.

Sabina MÜLLER Winterthur, Switzerland

moonlight -
snails dining á deux
  in the cat's bowl

winter pond,
leap - thud
a frog

Dorothy KENT Ewelme, Oxfordshire

from *The Spotted Unicorn*

On snowy evening
stopping by neighbour's dark woods
horse leaves steaming gift.

In forest of night
Panda! Panda! burning bright
Soon, bedroom carpet.

Sing of dappled things!
Freckled legs and pickled eggs
Budgies' wings. Nipples.

Roger McGOUGH London

in the lampshade
the soft detonation
of moths

John CAPP Warminster, Wiltshire

long after the child's gone
a silver balloon
playing on the ceiling

leaving, you forgot
to take the warmth
out of your handshake

Gabriel GRIFFIN Orta San Giulio, Italy

So lonely today.
Goldfish
gets an extra feed.

Terry CUTHBERT Oxford

the fridge clicks off -
cooing in the eaves,
doves

last night's stars
caught on my coat sleeve
goldenrod seeds

mud on the carpet -
mother becomes
a vacuum cleaner

chopped log -
ice glints
in its grain

battlesite...
blooming in the ditch,
forget-me-nots

they stayed when he left -
my brother's boots
filled with cobwebs

Mark RUTTER Surry, Maine

Blind Sister

conkers drop into her lap -
she holds them
for the first time

Cosmopolitan -
she turns the glossy pages
for their sound

footsteps...
she greets him by name
before he speaks

mother's face:
she has felt it age
in her hands

Mark RUTTER Surry, Maine

A storm.
Mother's body warms
naked little birds.

A mouse, pink footed,
scarcely walking
over the moss.

A gale. The branches
of the olive tree still hide
the most fragile birds.

Dejan BOGOJEVIC Valjevo, Yugoslavia

on and on she goes
the little Italian
nightingale

Lesley LENDRUM Linlithgow, Scotland

Nuns in Milan Cathedral

Disappearing in dark spaces
shunning the paparazzi light
they have the run of the place

it is their hallowed habitat
even the tattooed stained glass
shocks with its impertinence

growing neither young nor old
their skin has a slightly waxy look
candles burned up half their glow

not needing to be checked like us
for shorts or sleeveless t-shirts
they are like a quorum of magpies

even when I reach high numbers
their number always reverts to one
that singularity of sorrow.

Cherry blossoms falling -
a carp follows just below
a duck's wake

Pregnant cat's
eyes follow me
everywhere

With their voices
cicadas create the shape
of a big tree

Tsunehiko HOSHINO Tokyo, Japan

spring: bonsai leafburst;
    within my fatherly hands
        the forest's power

Choreography

Blows the Vardar.
Trees dance lamely, whisper for legs.
A dwarfish figure limps along
picking and picking up nothing.

Vardar - a wind blowing from the north into Thessaloniki

Yannis GOUMAS Halandri, Greece

the old pond
afterwards
echoless

Index of Poets

Other acorn titles include:

only when the sun shines brightly
by Magnus Mills

Magnus Mills caught the limelight when he became the first
bus driver to be short-listed for the Booker Prize.
His novel: 'The Restraint of Beasts' went on to sell over
30,000 copies and has been translated into 16 languages.
This is his first collection of short stories.

'each one a gem' - *Time Out*

'beautifully produced.' - *The Daily Telegraph*

80pp, A6, £3.99 ISBN 0 9534205 1 5

---

water
by Chris Mulhern

A haiku journey, each section corresponding to one aspect
of water - from snowmelt and cloud water to dry land.
His previous collection *cloud blunt moon* was first
published in 1994, and is now in its third edition.

water:
your seeking for dryness, for thirst
for all that is arid in me

'a book to be explored, to lose yourself in' - *Presence Magazine*

'filled with fine things' - *Lucien Stryk*

90 pp, A6, £4.99 ISBN 0 9534205 0 7
Illustrated with pen and ink sketches.

acorn book company

is an independent
publisher of small, high quality editions.

We also operate a mail order web-site
specialising in haiku and minimalist poetry.

For more information
please visit us at:
www.acornbook.co.uk

These and other titles are available direct from
acorn book company, PO Box 191, Tadworth,
Surrey KT20 5YQ. **Post free in the UK.**
Cheques payable to acorn book company.
or email your order to sales@acornbook.co.uk